When I Am *Older*,
I Will Pray More

When I Am *Older*, I Will Pray More

Prayers in the Senior Years

Roy K. Bohrer

iUniverse, Inc.
Bloomington

WHEN I AM OLDER, I WILL PRAY MORE
PRAYERS IN THE SENIOR YEARS

iUniverse books may be ordered through booksellers or by contacting:

iUniverse
1663 Liberty Drive
Bloomington, IN 47403
www.iuniverse.com
1-800-Authors (1-800-288-4677)

ISBN: 978-1-4620-3949-4 (sc)
ISBN: 978-1-4620-4040-7 (hc)
ISBN: 978-1-4620-4168-8 (ebk)

Library of Congress Control Number: 2011912583

Printed in the United States of America

iUniverse rev. date: 08/18/2011

Recommendations and Praises for
When I Am Older, I Will Pray More

Some come up with good ideas. Some gain superior insights. Some have a way with words. Roy Bohrer demonstrates in his cleverly worded collection of prayers that he excels in all three categories. Seniors will find that he has captured what they would wish to say to God in prayer.

The Reverend Dr. Ray F. Martens, former president of Concordia University Texas
Austin, Texas

****

What a treasure this book is, just like the author himself! The prayers are simple, yet profound. During the many years I served as the city of Austin's manager of Senior Programs, Roy Bohrer got involved in support of our programs and quickly became a voice for those who had none. Of even more value to us was his special heart and interest in seniors, always reaching out to the elderly in their time of need, counseling those who were troubled, rejoicing with those who had a new great-grandchild, or comforting those who were grieving. At a special recognition of his services to the community, I thanked him by using a quote from a line in a song: "And the angels must have sent you, for they meant you just for us." I still feel that way.

Gloria Mata Pennington, former manager, City of Austin Senior Programs
Austin, Texas

****

As a pastor, I always found joy in weaving words into liturgical prayers, but sincerely praying from my heart most often brought fumbling, mumbling, stumbling words that never seemed fitly framed together. Roy Bohrer has woven the warp and woof of timeless words into a tapestry of thoughtful, touching prayers for all occasions. I find his offering of piety and praise a significant and useful resource "for such a time [senior years] as this . . ."

The Reverend Dr. John R. Evans, HR minister member, Presbyterian Church (USA)
Dallas, Texas

****

As a result of meeting with and talking to many seniors, as well as my own life experiences, I know that these prayers speak to seniors' thoughts and feelings. In the sunset of life, we can be uplifted and renewed by these words of encouragement and enlightenment. Time is of the essence for a more meaningful life, and these affirming prayer thoughts can help to renew our todays and tomorrows!

Richard Nowery, volunteer for senior programs
Shreveport, Louisiana

****

Having served as a parish priest for over thirty years, ministering to many seniors in a variety of circumstances, I believe the themes and thoughts in these prayers that Roy Bohrer has written will be very helpful and meaningful in the lives of aging folks. The prayers are in a personal style with down-to-earth language. Not knowing any other prayer book produced especially for seniors, I am happy for a useful resource like this.

The Rev. Kirby D. Garner, Santa Cruz Catholic Church
Buda, Texas

****

What a marvelous prayer book! The prayers are short and specific for today's seniors. Finally, a book for so many of us who have a difficult time putting a prayer together. Roy has filled a need for our generation. The beauty of this book is that it can be adapted for any faith community. As a senior and a clinician, I recommend this book.

Lois VanLaningham, LCSW, retired medical social worker
Austin, Texas

****

Roy is a compassionate, kind-spirited, and humorous guy, and his clear prayers will touch the common man and woman. This small treasure of a prayer book will help us put ourselves into the hand of God again and again as we go through our ordinary and not-so-ordinary days. We resonate with the warmth and personal nature of these prayers, aimed at helping us to communicate with God on a wide variety of issues we face in our lives.

Bob and Sharon Moeller, assisting ministers, St. Hubert's Catholic Community
Chanhassen, Minnesota

****

I love my grandpa. He is real good at speaking and praying. All of us like to hear his prayers. I know he has always been very nice to older people, and now he is a grandpa himself! You will like his prayers in this book.

Samantha Marie Bohrer, age 7
Wimberley, Texas

Contents

Dedicated to everyone
who has ever prayed for me

Preface

It is good to remember that prayer is not so much an act of communication or a verbal exercise as it is a position, a posture for life. Mother Teresa once wrote, "Prayer is not asking. Prayer is putting oneself in the hands of God, at his disposition, and listening to his voice in the depths of our hearts."

From my own prayer experience, as well as my experience as a pastor who listened to church members for many years, I know that praying often gets neglected. We do not pray in a way or as often as we would like. The two most common problems cited are lack of knowing how to pray and lack of time to pray. This prayer book aims to help with those problems and has been written especially for seniors. I wrote these prayers from the perspective of a senior and a former minister; they are intended as prayers for those in their older years. In searching bookstore shelves, I did not find prayer books written especially for those in their senior years. None provided easy illustrations, actual prayers, and usable examples of how to pray for this growing segment of the population. Most people in their later years are retired or at least working fewer hours, so lack of time isn't really a concern for the intended users of this book—those who have fewer things to do and more time for spiritual meditation and prayer. I hope you will find these prayers useful for your life and inspirational for making up your own prayers and that your spiritual life will be more fruitful.

These prayers are not intended for certain religious faiths or groups; they are generally usable by all. You will not find certain forms that you may have been taught as appropriate for your faith or that you are accustomed to using, such as the common Christian closing, "in Jesus's name." You may want to add closings, openings, addresses, other formats or language, or alternate days or occasions in order to make these prayers more comfortable for you within your own faith.

Prayer is the lifeline of the divine relationship, a relationship that is truly "made in heaven." In the senior years, when things seem to be—and often are—slipping away, maintaining relationships is vital. When facing the closing of earthly life and whatever may be ahead, a relationship with the divine is of supreme importance. It is my hope that these prayers will help to maintain your relationship lifeline to the divine.

You, Lord, are my inheritance;
you give me all I need.
My future is in your hands.
How wonderful are your gifts to me,
what a good inheritance!
(from Psalm 16)

Let Us Pray

Legend has it that a poetry contest was held each year in the ancient world. The third-place winner would receive a silver rose. The second-place winner would receive a gold rose. And the first-place winner would receive a real, living rose—a beautiful, fragrant, living rose—that soon, of course, would wilt, dry up, and die. Despite what naturally happens, who would not choose the living rose above all?

The privilege of living life is to be prized, cherished, enjoyed, and celebrated, in spite of the weaknesses, sorrows, and tragedies that befall all of us and in spite of the inevitable wilting, drying up, and dying.

Let us pray . . .

Prayers for Me

How Did I Get This Old?

I look into a mirror, Lord, and am surprised. I think, *How did I get to be this old?* The time flew by, and the years piled up. Now look at me! Maybe it's not so bad. The years have been your gift, Lord, and I did what I did, right or wrong. Forgive me for everything that was wrong and continue to encourage me in what is right. I think of the old German saying, "We get too soon old and too late smart." Thank you for what I learned along the way. Thank you for memories, Lord, because they comfort me, entertain me, and encourage me. I have no idea how many more years I have here, but keep me from becoming discouraged about growing old, because age really is a blessing. No matter that I might look different; I am still pretty good—and I know that I am good in your eyes. Amen.

Roy K. Bohrer

Not Another Year Like the Last One

I cannot take another year like the last one, Lord. It had too much evil to fight, too much trouble to face, too many burdens to bear. Why me, Lord? Why so much? I know these are meaningless questions for which there are no human answers, but they come to me in my times of trial and weakness. There is no way I could have made it without your strength and abiding presence. Forgive me for doubts and fears, Lord, and keep me going into the future. Spare me from many troubles so that I am not defeated or overwhelmed by any kind of enemies, and give me a positive stronghold on life. Lord, give me the faith and the resources to be secure and to be a survivor. But please . . . not another year like the last one. Amen.

For Faith

It seems, Lord, that I can see more clearly now that a person needs a strong faith to survive. Maybe life is more complicated, maybe life has more tensions and troubles, or maybe it just seems that way to me, but without a strong faith, I think I would crumble and fall. I need to have the assurance of faith that the world is in your hands, Lord, and that your power is stronger than everything else. Give me a strong faith every day! When I feel threatened, when I am being cheated, when I see the terrible actions of people, or when I hear about crimes, victims, and tragedies, I need faith, Lord, to go forward and to keep going. When my health, my location, my bank account, my leaders, my friends, or my family give me disappointments or challenges, I need faith to keep going. Please do not let anything weaken my faith in you, and do not allow anyone to scare me into faithlessness. Amen.

For Comfort

I know life is not easy, and I know that the senior years, especially, bring some uncomfortable situations. Although it is normal, Lord, let the discomfort that I feel be softened and eased so that I can function peacefully. Help me to be comfortable so that I can rise to the occasion and act in a way that will be God-pleasing, good for me, and helpful to others. Let me feel the steadying support of your strong hand to calm me and buoy me up. I know that I have been wonderfully made and that I am your child. Give me the comforting assurance that all things will work together for good. I need not be embarrassed, afraid, ashamed, worried, depressed, or uncomfortable in any way, as I know there is no problem or situation that can take me from your love and mercy. I breathe deeply and confidently with your Spirit's comforting presence. Amen.

I Feel So Tired

Lord, I feel so tired. I don't know if I am sick, if I am depressed, if I haven't had enough rest, or if I have just run out of energy, but I don't like to feel so tired. I need to renew my energy and my strength in order to do the things I need to do, because I just cannot stay in bed and do nothing. Help me to get hold of myself and get renewing rest, O Lord. Give me sound sleep. Heal me of my infirmities. Help me to relax. Bring me out of whatever is dragging me down. If it is good for me, lead me to figure out what my problems and weaknesses are right now so that I can work on fixing them. Let me dwell on the positive things and on the blessings of life so that I can be fit for whatever the next day will bring. The victory over evil has been won; now let me rejoice in that victory and claim it for my life. Amen.

I Am Facing Surgery

I know it happens to almost everyone, but I don't like to have surgery; I don't like its risks and pains and questions. Help me, Lord, to face this time of surgery realistically and bravely. It is normal and expected that I would have some fears, but help me to be optimistic and strong and to keep the positives on top. Like any other time of my life, with the dangers and questions that come with each day, I will be in your hands, Lord, during this surgery. Guide the decisions and the work of the doctors and nurses so that this surgery will come out just the way it should, according to your knowledge and plan. According to your will, make this a successful surgery, Lord, so that good will come of it. Give me strength to bear the pain and whatever hardships there may be. I have to trust in you, Lord, and rest in your love. Amen.

My Recuperation

Thank you for helping me and the doctors and medical attendants to come through my illness and/or surgery, Lord. Now I look forward to healing and regaining strength. Sometimes recuperation can be long and tough, with many challenges, but I ask you to spare me the difficulties, Lord, and give me speedy and complete healing. I know that it is not your original divine will that your children should suffer at all, but we brought that upon ourselves with sinfulness. Help me, day by day, to fight the evil and the negatives and to push forward in your love and healing grace. These probably will be some long and difficult days, and I pray that you will give me patience and strength to keep me moving toward healing. I want to be well just as quickly as possible, Lord. Stay close to me to grant me that blessing. Amen.

For Health

With the increasing years come more weaknesses and challenges to my good health of body and mind. They call it aging. It hits all people in different ways and with different force, and I know I cannot expect to feel younger and healthier. But support me, Lord, so that I can maintain my health and fight off handicaps as much as possible. Give me the willpower to work on keeping healthy. Give me the right attitude to strive for physical, mental, and spiritual health. Push me however I need to be pushed. It might be exercise; it might be medication; it might be therapy; it might be doctors' visits; it might be diet; it might be changes in lifestyle. Whatever is needed, Lord, show it to me and enable me. I cannot conquer all weakness, but help me to believe strongly in my partnership with you, Lord, to give me success in maintaining health in these senior years. Amen.

For Strength

I can think of times in my life when I felt very strong, O Lord. Sometimes I thought I knew where my strength came from, and sometimes I didn't have a clue. Now I am confident that all strength ultimately comes from you, Lord, even though it may come through other humans or earthly endeavors. You are the source of strength. However you can keep me strong, whoever you can use to help me, and whatever process it may take, please, Lord, give me the strength to face today, this week, this year, and the rest of my life. The living isn't always so easy, even after all these years—perhaps especially after all these years. I want to be just as strong as I possibly can; I do not want to be weak. What it takes to be strong comes from you, Lord: faith, courage, hope, power, love, endurance, and knowledge. Grant me those blessings, I pray. Amen.

In Financial Worries

The best plans I can make to take care of myself financially still have many questions and possible pitfalls. The economies of this land and this world are not always secure. Give me patience and freedom from worry, Lord, as I think about my finances. Calm me with the assurance that the birds of the field are in your hands and the hairs of our heads are numbered, so we need not fret or worry. Enable me to make good decisions—wise and realistic—and then to go forward with confidence. Provide me with advisors and professionals who are trustworthy. When I need to make adjustments, let me see them, and help me make them. Let me see where I can be charitable and generous, as I want to be but not to my own downfall. Do not let me become grumpy, stingy, or totally consumed with money, but help me to be balanced. Especially help me to see good answers as I go along in your grace. Amen.

Contemplating a Change or Move

As we grow older, we dislike change more than ever. We need security, and the old and familiar usually gives us less fear and less worry. Forgive me, Lord, that I act weak and faithless about this coming change in my life. Something different is coming up; a change is coming. Maybe it will be difficult; maybe it will be easier than I think. Maybe it will be a blessing; maybe it will take hard work on my part. With your help, I know I can do it. Nothing is impossible with the Lord. Help me to have the right attitude and to emphasize the positive. I have made a choice to change (or someone else has decided it for me), so now remind me daily that I am not forsaken. All things can work together for good to those who love the Lord. Quiet my insides, and let my outside bring forth faith. Amen.

I Feel Lonely

No one in faith is ever alone, but right now I am feeling lonely, without the presence of someone else with me. I know that there are people who are interested in me and who care about me, but now it is hard for me to remember that others care, because I feel as if I need more. I need someone; I need reassurance. Lord, help me not to dwell on that human presence that I want, that hand I think I need, that caring heart I want physically close to me, or that attention that I'd like. Remind me constantly of the closeness of your love, the care of your divine plans, and the warmth of hearts that are joined in love, even though they are not present. Every other believer is actually my friend and my companion. Let me take joy from that. Help me to practice feeling the reassurance of others who are not with me. And work on me, Lord, to get rid of loneliness by reaching out to others—those I can reach, whether in spirit and inner concern or physically—whoever they are. I know the best antidote for my loneliness is for me to give of myself to someone else and forget about my feelings of need. There might be lonelier people than I who are not far away from me, and we all can be blessed. Amen.

Traveling

Sometimes I feel I cannot get around now as well as I used to. Those times when I travel call for special protection and help in these older years. When I am traveling, I often get more nervous. I worry about new things and changes, and I fret about those things that I cannot do well but that might be expected of me. Grant me your assuring presence, Lord, in my travels. Let me know that I can make it and that if I make mistakes, it won't matter much. If I am slower, who cares? If I am late, or off schedule, or have to change plans, that is not the end of the world. Keep me calm and patient in my traveling. Let your abiding presence give me safety in my travels, because there are certainly dangers. So many people are involved with traveling. Grant the blessings of skill and responsible action to all so that we all may be protected along the way. Go with me all the way, Lord. Amen.

My Disability

Sometimes when I think of the disability that I have and look around at other people who seem to be whole and unencumbered, I feel depressed and angry. I ask "Why me, Lord?" Sometimes I notice that others have bigger problems and greater disabilities than I do, and I am thankful for who I am and what I have. Lord, I want to focus more on what I have and not pay attention to what I do not have. Help me to have a thankful heart and a strong faith so that I can live in a positive way, overcoming my disability. I do not know why this disability was allowed to come to me, but I need the confidence that you have not forsaken me and will be my constant help and guide. Life itself is precious, and all lives are tainted in some way because of the wickedness in the world. Do not let my problems weigh me down to ruin my life. Lord, remind me that you are my rock and fortress through everything. Amen.

Thinking of My Own Death

As I read the obituaries regularly now and as the years keep passing by, I cannot help but think of my own time of death. Lord, help me not to be morbid but to be realistic about my passing out of this earthly life. Help me not to be frightened or worried but to be faithful and confident that I will be with you forever—that is really what matters. I am sure it is for a good reason that you have given us so little information on what it is like to die, on how we should view our time here—or lack of time—and what the afterlife is really like. I have so many questions and so few answers; I have only your word of assurance. I also know that no one can know the time, place, or manner of passing. I ask, Lord, that my death not come in some terrible way but that it will be easy and peaceful for me and for others with me. People talk about being ready. I am thankful that I know your love, O Lord, your forgiveness, and your way of salvation, and so I am spiritually ready. Lead me to make decisions and to take legal, financial, and planning actions that will make me more ready to depart this life in an earthly way as well. If it be your will, grant to me a long, satisfying life and then take me safely home. Amen.

I Am Worried

As much as I know of your assurance not to worry, and I think of the birds of the air and the lilies of the field who do not worry, my emotions get the best of me—and I worry, Lord. I worry because I do not know what lies ahead. I worry because I cannot control the situation. I worry because there might be suffering. I worry that I will not be able to do something I need to do. I worry that I might be blamed. I worry about mistakes. Forgive me, Lord, for my weakness that leads to these worries. I am faced with worldly concerns, and I dwell on them instead of realizing that in the long run, they do not matter. Assure me that it is not a requirement that I worry and that it is not careless to be calm and unworried. Teach me more and more that the grace you give me to live under, your mercy and love to cleanse me, and your peace to surpass all human conditions are all that matters. Ease my poor little mind and heart, O Lord, with your Spirit. Amen.

Feeling a Loss

I feel the pain of this loss, Lord, because it is humanly normal as we journey through life to tie our hearts and lives to certain people or things, and then we suffer pain when we lose them. I am hurting now, Lord. You, O Lord, know the pain and suffering of losses; what I feel now is well known to you. I know that it is not wrong of me to feel disappointment, defeat, loss, or emptiness, but keep me from letting this loss overshadow all of life and its blessings or your loving claim on me. Let me not become bitter, as those do who have no spiritual grounding, and let me not become cynical or hateful, as those do who do not have your love. Let the passing of time be my friend that helps in healing from this loss. Lift me up, in your time, O Lord, to show me the brightness of blessings. Amen.

I Want to be Pleasant, Lord

The little prayer "Lord, keep your arm around my shoulder and your hand over my mouth" is what I often need these days. Lord, I do not want to be a grumpy old person, but it's so easy to be that. I don't know if the changes in the world or the changes in me are more to blame, but I really do not like a great deal of what is happening around me. Help me not to be a grumpy old person! Show me how to reflect on good blessings that come to me, good likeable people around me, and good things happening in the world. Teach me that I am not in charge of the world or the actions of others. I am not responsible for training everyone else in my ways. I want to be known as a pleasant person, Lord, so lead me in the pathways of forgiveness and joy. Support me in my weaknesses, and help me to speak in a positive way for healing and building up, not tearing down. Amen.

I Want to Understand, Lord

The passing years have brought many changes in the world, in our society, and in people. I have welcomed many changes, Lord, and I thank you for the enjoyment of new blessings. I also have changed over time, but some things I cannot understand or accept, and that causes problems for me and others. Help me to put the best construction on things and to try to understand them, Lord, so that I may serve your purposes and act as a member of your blessed family. Help me to discern evil and wrongdoing and separate it from my own selfishness or lack of understanding. I do not want to stand up for what is wrong, but I do want to support what is right in the world, so give me the gift of distinguishing them. I need the courage to admit my own failures and weaknesses and the ability to understand the actions and motives of others. As long as I am in this world, Lord, I want to be an instrument for good. Help me. Amen.

Making the Right Decision

Okay, Lord, I have to decide. What will it be? Lead me in some way to the right decision; show me the right answer. I have thought about all the possibilities and the consequences. I think that I know what each way would mean. I have thought about the pros and the cons. Please bring me more enlightenment very soon if I have missed something. I am ready to decide, but I want to make sure that you are guiding me, Lord, and that what I decide is your will. I am calling on your presence and your help, and I am turning this over to you. Influence me and lead me to make the best decision so that when I make my choice, I will know that it is what it should be. Give me confidence in my decision, Lord; I know that I have not made it alone. You are beside me and in me as my helper and leader, and we can go forward in peace. Amen.

My Feelings Are Hurt

I am sad, Lord, because my feelings have been hurt. Human relationships can be complicated and fragile. No matter whose fault it is, Lord, and no matter who intended what, I need to ask for your strength and guidance to get me through these feelings of hurt. When I am feeling sorry for myself I cannot live in the right way. Help me to figure out whether I need to apologize and whether I need to take action. Help me to know what I should say or not say so that I can restore a relationship that is now hurting. Let me be forgiving. Let me listen. Let me be brave. Let me boldly speak the truth, if that is what is called for. Help me to swallow my pride, if that is necessary for healing. I only know that hurt feelings are a weakness and a burden that interferes in my spiritual life with you and in my life with others. I want to come out of this. Bless me in your mercy and support. Amen.

Help Me to Forgive

So long ago I learned "Forgive us our trespasses as we forgive those who trespass against us." So long ago I learned about your forgiveness, O Lord, as the key to my relationship of peace with you forever, and I cherish that forgiveness. But when it comes to my forgiving others, sometimes there is a blockage. It is obviously my stubborn weakness and sinfulness that stand in the way of forgiving others, even when I know I am forgiven freely and fully in your mercy. After these many years of living with and relating to others, I still need help with this, O Lord. Break the blockage within me; break the stubborn resistance to forgiveness that I should freely and fully grant to others. Every other person has weaknesses, makes mistakes, is affected by sin, and is capable of evil, intentionally or unintentionally. Soften my hardness of heart, Lord, to make me willing to grant forgiveness, even without an apology or explanation from the other person, just as I have known from your love. As you have forgiven me, O Lord, let me forgive. Amen.

For Forgiveness

The reformer Martin Luther had great insight when he wrote that a believer is justified and is completely forgiven in the eyes of God by faith, even as he remains a sinner. Even though we are washed clean from the eternal effects of sin, there is still evil in our nature and in our world that will lead us to sin. We are not perfect in this life, although we appear as perfect in the eyes of God. I am far from perfect! Therefore, I beg you, Lord, to forgive my natural sinfulness and forgive my sinful actions. Forgive me especially for those evil things that seem to come easily and often to me—my particular weaknesses. Forgive me that I cannot conquer or change certain bad things about me, no matter how hard I try or how often I regret them. Forgive me, Lord, for the sins that I know and those I do not recognize or remember. Let me know that your forgiveness totally blankets me, Lord, so that if I should die without a chance to speak repentance or ask forgiveness, I still have the assurance that I am totally forgiven and acceptable in your sight. Amen.

For Peacefulness

So often, peace is mentioned in the scriptures as the ultimate blessing, and I believe that it is. Thinking back through the years, I know the times of special peace were the best times for me. Peace can only come from above, from trusting in your love, O Lord, as you grant your people total comfort and joy. I pray for that peace in my life, for peaceful contentment in my heart, and for peace between people, peace in families, peace among nations, peace in the midst of danger, and peace in the place of turmoil. It is all ultimately peace from you, O Lord, as you work through people and situations and in our spirits. Peace means freedom from guilt, freedom from threat, freedom from fear, and freedom from harm. The scriptures call it the peace that passes all human understanding—the peace from above that is beyond human reason. Bring peace to me and my life, O Lord, especially if there is anything trying to interfere with that peace right now. Amen.

I Am Disappointed

Try as hard as I might to be positive, thoughtful, considerate, and forgiving, I get disappointed by the actions of others. When things do not go as I wished, when results do not come as I expected, when performance is not as anticipated, or when the end is not what I assumed, I am disappointed and downhearted. Forgive my selfishness, Lord, in thinking that things should always be as I want. Help me to change my mind, Lord, and make me forgiving toward others whose deeds are not as I hoped. Make me an instrument for change and for improvement, to help others whose failures lead to disappointment for them and for me. Help us to set realistic goals. Let me see that disappointment about small matters is not significant in the big picture of life so that I may keep the perspective of total living by faith in you, Lord. Amen.

Roy K. Bohrer

Fearful of the Future

Even though I know that you have the whole world in your hands, Lord, sometimes I lose sight of your promises, as I am overcome by fears, threats, and worries every day. It seems as if fears for the future of the world, for our nation, and for humanity are more prevalent now than they were years ago—maybe that is because I am older and more alert to those fears. Evil is certainly as rampant as it always has been, but you have won the victory over all evil powers for eternity, Lord. No matter what happens, we are not to fear. Forgive me, Lord, for my fears and worries, as though I have no faith. Remind me that your will is not always the will of people, and your ways are not the ways of the world. Help me and all people to be responsible citizens of this world that you have given us and to call upon you for divine guidance. Whatever the future is, it belongs to you, O Lord, and I will be with you forever. Amen.

Guide Me, Lord

Having lived many years, I have experienced and learned many things, Lord, but I still need to call upon you for divine guidance. I do not know all things, do not understand all things, and cannot do all things. I come to you for help, Lord, because I do not know what to do. Please show me the way, give me the answer, lead me to see the truth, and let me know your will. In some way, clearly give me the guidance I seek, Lord, so that I may be assured that what I do is right. If I need to make a decision, work in my thinking so that my decision is correct. If it is someone else's action, guide that person in doing what should be done. If it depends on circumstances coming together, work in those things, Lord, so that all will be as it should be. Give me assurance, peace, and rest in your guidance. Amen.

Oh, Lord, How I Miss Him/Her

Although losing loved ones and grieving are a part of life, especially in one's elder years, it hurts, Lord. Oh, how I miss this loved one! I want to be brave. I want to be strong. I want to be seen as full of faith, but you know, Lord, how lonely I feel and how much I hate making the adjustment to life without this one I have loved for so long. Give me peace and comfort, Lord, so that I may rejoice in the good memories and in the loving family and friendships that are still with me. The passage of time takes away some sooner than others—we don't know why—but those who are left here in this world still have time to live, time to love, and time to serve. And time is a good friend that can soften the feelings of loss and wipe away the emptiness. Help me to know that my loss is real, and it will not soon go away. Still, I will go forward in your peace and reassurance. Amen.

For Sleep

Lord, I am so frustrated with myself when I cannot get a good night's sleep. I don't know why it has happened to me more often lately, but either I cannot fall asleep when I go to bed, or I wake up and cannot get back to sleep. Help me to relax, Lord. Give me peacefulness for my sleeping. There is nothing I can do about solving problems or finishing chores while I am sleeping; help me let go of things when it is time for sleeping. Let me develop a peaceful, blessed assurance that will enable my body and mind to get the rest I need. Lead me to a way to relax—mental images or word repetition, a thought process, or a feeling of strong trust in your love—that will help me to sleep. It is not the end of the world if I have trouble sleeping sometimes, Lord, but please grant me the blessing of enough healthy sleep most of the time. Amen.

Prayers for Others

For Someone Who Doesn't Seem to Like Me

I am not sure, Lord, whether the actions and signals I am getting from someone indicate that I have done something wrong, but I feel rejected. I don't want to be unaccepted or disliked. When I search my mind for what I might have said or done to another to cause trouble, I cannot come up with an answer. But forgive me, Lord, for anything that made me the cause of friction, and lead me and this other person to be forgiving toward each other. Open up the pathways for peace between us, and show me how I can be an instrument of whatever healing needs to take place. Help me to do whatever it takes to say and do the right things for us to accept one another in our relationship. If there isn't a problem—if I am wrong about my feelings—let me see and feel the acceptance. I know, Lord, that not everyone will like everything I say or do, nor will everyone want to be my friend. But I do not like to be rejected outright. Help me to find peace. Amen.

For My Adult Children

Lord, those you gave me to nurture, train, and prepare for life stay close to my heart and are prominently on my mind throughout life, so they are also in my prayers. Thank you for the gift of my children, Lord, for they have brought so many blessings to me. Even though they have grown up, their heartaches still hurt me, their worries still bother me, their decisions still weigh on me, and their joys are still my happiness. Thank you, dear Lord, for all of the good things my children have, and keep them thankful to you. Give them wisdom, peacefulness, and faith for living so that they may stay close to you and honor you. Whatever troubles they have, whatever conflicts interrupt them, whatever threats come to them, sustain them, Lord, and help them to figure things out in the best way. Do not forsake them or leave them. Give them satisfaction and keep them in the joy of the Lord. This is a parent's humble plea. Amen.

For My Grandchildren

As little ones have always been dear to you, Lord, keep my grandchildren safe and secure in your love. Help them in the many stages they have yet to go through and the many things they do not know. Help them with the many temptations they have not yet had, the many decisions they have not yet faced, and the many years they have not yet seen. According to your will, give them long, peaceful, and joyful lives that they may know the contentment of your love. Make them blessings to their parents and all to whom they relate. Continue to give to them good experiences and valuable training so that they may develop in every way into healthy adults. May they grow up to be good citizens, responsible workers, and faithful members of your kingdom, with inner satisfaction and outward stability. Long after I am gone, let their memories of me be a positive strength for them. Amen.

For My Spouse/Partner/Loved One

What a great blessing you have given me, Lord, in the companionship of that one who is closest to me, my partner in this life. I thank you, Lord, for bringing us together, for all the great things we have shared, and for the continuation of our love. Through the years, I have often been the cause of disappointment, heartache, and confusion for my partner. Forgive me for all of those times. Help my partner and me to bask in the healing power of your love and mercy. Give to my partner health, satisfaction, peacefulness, and the joy that passes all human understanding. You know better than I do the special needs my partner has right now. Please, dear Lord, let your presence be the needed comfort, let your promises be the needed healing, and let your power be the needed strength. If it is according to your will, give us many more years of companionship and love so that we may continue to share together whatever life brings. Amen.

For a Friend Who Is Alone

I know that people were not meant to be alone and yet in this imperfect world, loneliness is one of the saddest burdens. Today, I am especially thinking about my friend who is all alone at this time and feels a burden of loneliness. Let the promise of your presence be a comfort. Help my friend to develop an inner strength from the faith that your Spirit sustains in our prayer life, in worship, in the reading of your Word, and in the meditation on your presence. And then, Lord, let there be other persons, including me, who can help lift the loneliness. Open up my friend to the company of others at every chance. Show me how and when I can be of help. Let us have meaningful contacts, good visits, and important times of sharing so that my friend's loneliness will be less and less of a problem. And then, let times alone be felt as a blessing and not a burden. Amen.

For a Friend's Health

Sickness comes into life as an intrusion. It attacks our bodies and tortures our spirits. My friend is under attack now, Lord, and needs your help. Beyond the doctors, nurses, therapists, and caregivers, I know that your power can do anything. Healing is what we would like to have, Lord—complete and speedy healing, if it be your will. I ask for your guidance of the medical staff in their healing work. I realize that we do not understand everything, and we do not know the time and place appointed for the exercise of your special and miraculous power. I leave it in your hands and in your will, Lord. There is no greater love than your love. There is no better place to rest than in your arms. There is no stronger assurance than the promise of your mercy and presence. Be with my friend, O Lord, with all of your blessings. Amen.

For the World

"This Is My Song," written by Lloyd Stone, reminds us: "Other hearts in other lands are beating with hopes and dreams as true and high as mine . . . skies are everywhere as blue as mine . . . Oh hear my song, O God of all the nations, a song of peace for their land and for mine." Lord, you have made a great world and wonderful people to populate it, but sinfulness in many forms has caused enmity, suffering, heartache, and hardship. The warring nations, so full of sin, include all of the nations of the world. Help the nations to overcome evil and to seek peace. Enable leaders all over the world to strive for peacefulness, cooperation, and the end of fighting. There is enough for everyone, Lord; let them see that and hold that truth. Make our nation a good example of peace, sharing, and love of humanity. Let people everywhere realize the beauty of the world, the opportunities for good, and the blessings of your love. Amen.

For Family Members and Friends

Lord, I believe there are four important things in life; I pray for these things for all of my dear ones and most especially for the one who is in my heart right now: Give spiritual faith, O Lord—strong, sustaining, meaningful faith for living. Give health, O Lord—not perfect but good health, so the trials and tribulations and the ins and outs of daily life can be embraced successfully. Give satisfactory work, O Lord, so that there is a fulfilling job to be done, joy in accomplishments, and acceptable payment and rewards. Give peacefulness, O Lord—the blanket that should cover all the days and nights, in all relationships and all encounters, in comings and goings, the peace that reassures and upholds. These four, O Lord, faith and health and work and peace, are my prayer for all of them, that their lives may be full and blessed and good. Amen.

For Our Nation

I am thankful that our country has been blessed beyond measure with many freedoms, opportunities, and material riches. What a wonderful life you have given us here, O Lord, although we are not in the least worthy of so many blessings. Help me and all citizens to see how blessed we are, to realize the value of those blessings, and to be dedicated to responsibly and thankfully using what you have given. We know there are dangers to our nation from the outside and from the inside, and although we do not deserve the goodness we have had, I pray that you will continue to bless our people and our land with freedom, opportunity, and safety. Keep war from coming to our land. Within our borders, help us to sort out how to treat all people fairly, how to care for all people, and how to welcome others while still protecting our citizens. Economic problems, spiritual depravities, selfishness, greed, and hatred all threaten our nation from within. We need your guidance, your power, and your love, O Lord. Whoever our leaders are and whatever they may think or say or promise, please let your will be done for our nation, and give your help to us. Amen.

For Someone Having Surgery

Our lives are always in your hands, Lord, and every day we need your love and grace and care, but surgery brings an abnormal intrusion into a person's life. It can cause the patient to have very frightening and serious thoughts about what could happen and about living or dying. Please be with this person facing surgery now, O Lord, with an extra measure of faith, peacefulness, confidence, and hope—and an extra measure for the day of surgery because of the dangers that are involved. Attend this surgery, Lord, along with all of the medical staff who will be there, so that your divine plan can be fulfilled and your holy will be done. I pray this surgery will be successful so that better health may soon follow. I pray this surgery will accomplish what is intended without complications or mistakes. Bring a speedy healing after the surgery—and all treatments. Sustain the medical staff with skill and confidence in their important decisions and actions. It is normal for such a critical time to bring attention to the frailty of our lives and the importance of our health, and it is not wrong to ponder the meaning of life and the certainty of death. Grant to this person having surgery and all of the family and friends who are worried a reassurance of your love and protecting presence. I commit all of them to your merciful care. Amen.

For My Doctor

Thank you, Lord, for providing me with other people to help my life, especially professional people like my doctor. I cannot study everything. I cannot know everything. I cannot do everything. I have to trust my doctor for medical care. Give my doctor the insight and wisdom necessary to diagnose my troubles correctly and to decide the correct procedures and treatments. I know that your will is done through people, and your power is shown through human instruments. I place myself in your hands, Lord, through trusting in my doctor's care. Give me confidence in dealing with medical issues I do not understand, because I am calling upon your loving care. Amen.

Roy K. Bohrer

For My Faith Community

From the beginning, Lord, you have said it is not good for us to be alone. Through the centuries, you have shown your people the blessings of being together with others—gatherings for spiritual worship, growth in faith, and strength in life. We are blessed to this day with the opportunities and joys of being in a community of faith. Thank you, Lord, for the growth and strength of gathering together for study, worship, fellowship, and service to others. An older person, especially, needs support, so thank you, Lord, for giving me a spiritual home for sharing. Put your blessing on what we do together so that our intentions are sincere, our teachings are right, and our actions are good. In this way will many be blessed within our group. Give us the desire and commitment to reach out to others. Give us the resources to be a faithful and strong community of your people, with good leadership and dedicated service. Amen.

For the Baby I Saw Today

I have seen countless people during the days of my life. I do not know many of them, but they still should be my concern. I can't help but think of the little baby I saw today, Lord, because my heart was moved by that new life. I ask the blessing of your love and mercy for that child. I have lived many years, and I know what life can bring. That baby has no idea of the joys of goodness and threats of evil that might come; nor do I. But the child needs to know you, Lord, and needs to know the joy of salvation and the peace that passes human understanding. Whoever that baby is, wherever that baby will go, and however that baby will develop, Lord, let your hand of blessing and grace rest on the child throughout life, granting safety, faith, and peace. Amen.

For Someone in Danger

Although we are always surrounded by many dangers—the forces of evil and the intent of wickedness are a constant threat—I am concerned, Lord, with the danger to the person on my mind now. Please reach out with your protection, your safety, your defense, and your help. O Lord, your power is greater than any other. Your love is sure, and your victory over evil and danger is proven and clear. Maybe the danger is great, or maybe it is not so serious, but whatever it is, Lord, I know your presence is important and needed. Let your sure defense win over dangerous threats, and give protection and victory to this person. Bring your love and surrounding arms of tender care to the mind and heart of this person and anyone affected by the danger. Let the knowledge that our times are in your hands be the faith that sustains and the confidence that wins. We all must rest ourselves in you. Amen.

For My Neighbors

I see some of my neighbors frequently, but other neighbors I hardly see at all. They all are your children, Lord, created by you for life in this world. Help me to be interested and concerned about them, Lord, even if I do not know them very well. Let me be helpful when I can. Let me be loving and considerate when I can. When you bring them close to me, push me to befriend them, as someone who cares about them and their lives. I pray for all of them today, Lord, asking a special blessing on each one of them. Whatever their needs, whatever their concerns, and whatever their joys, be with them. Give each of them the faith to know they belong to you and your family and the incentive to put their trust in you, above all. Help them to put down evil and resist temptation that will bring them to destructive lifestyles and unhappy conclusions. Work in their lives to keep them safe and happy. Let us be good neighbors together in this place. Amen.

Roy K. Bohrer

For My Pet

You, Lord, have provided me with the companionship and joy of my pet. I would be lonely on many days without this creature that shares my home and my life. I thank you that you have brought us together for good. People have different opinions about the life and mind and soul of a pet, but it doesn't matter to me. I know that I love this pet, and the pet loves me, and we share good times and our life together. This animal is a special joy to me. I enjoy providing for and taking care of it, and this pet seems to have affection for me. Please keep my pet safe and healthy, and help me to take proper care of it. Do not let me be unrealistic by failing to acknowledge that it is an animal pet and not another human being. Thank you for the life I share with my pet, and keep us together as long as possible. Amen.

For Someone Who Is Grieving

The pain of a loss hurts, and you know well, Lord, how we can suffer in grief. It is another of those sad things that came into our lives and your perfect world through our acceptance of evil and all of its consequences. Into the pain of this loss, which hurts so much, bring the assurance of your final and eternal victory and the peacefulness of your love, which nothing can ever destroy or take away. Let your gentle love lift up the grieving heart, dry the tears, and instill comfort and peace. Where there is sadness, let there be renewing hope. There is a time to grieve—it is good and natural—but Lord, in your mercy and in your right time, grant a bridge to healing. Ease the pain and the feeling of loss so that it does not go beyond what might be expected or what is normal. Keep this grieving person in your care. Amen.

For Someone Who Is Dying

Life and death are in your hands, O Lord. It saddens me that a life I know seems to be coming to an end. We learned long ago to pray "Thy will be done," and that is my prayer now, as none of us can know the divine will that controls all things and sets the time of life and death. If it would be your will, Lord, to keep this life in the world and to grant relief from suffering with healing for the body, please let your power come to keep this person alive. But if the time has come for the end of this person's life, then I acknowledge your will, Lord. I ask for an end to the sufferings of this world. I ask for a quiet release for this person, a comfortable ending, and peace at the last. Receive this person into the endless time of eternity. Give comfort and reassurance to all who are distraught by this impending loss, that their hearts may be consoled in your mercy and peace. Amen.

For Our Governmental Leaders

These are not easy times for the leadership of our nation; there are so many threats and conflicts within and beyond our borders. You have been Lord of all nations throughout history, even as nations have risen and fallen, some claiming godliness and some ungodliness. I pray that your power and your will may be sought by the governmental leaders of our nation at all levels. I pray that we may live under the assurance that they will call upon your name and that their trust is in you. Give your strong arm of guidance to those who lead our cities, states, and nation, whether they call upon you or do not. Give your strong arm of support to uphold our leaders. Grant wisdom, courage, and insight to them that decisions made and actions taken may bring results according to your holy will. Bless us as a nation that fears the Lord. Amen.

Roy K. Bohrer

For Spiritual Leaders

People of God need faithful leaders to reaffirm the scriptures and to point to the truth. We need them to uphold godliness in society, to teach us how to live better, and to set good examples of walking with the Lord. Provide honest and faithful spiritual leaders for our communities, Lord, that the people may be inspired and that you may be glorified. Enable all my spiritual leaders to have wisdom, patience, and steadfastness that they may perform their callings well, be witness to what is godly and good, and be faithful servants to your will. Strengthen them, uphold them, and comfort them in their times of weakness, temptation, and discouragement that they may not lose the faith. Grant a harvest of kingdom success to their proclamation and their witness. Amen.

For the Homeless, the Hungry, the Indigent

I know that it is the high calling of faith to provide food, drink, shelter, and help to those in need. There are so many needy in our world, Lord. I cannot understand why I am so blessed and others are not. It is not fair or right; it is a result of evil in humanity and throughout the world. Lord, empower me to help others more than I do, and help me to sort out the truly needy from the deceitful and lazy. It is not my responsibility to judge, but I want my assistance to be used for good. Enable me to make the right decisions about helping. When I cannot physically help, remind me, O Lord, to say a prayer for that indigent one, that hungry one, that homeless one whom I see. Give me a compassionate heart, Lord, to reach out to others—the children, the elderly, and everyone in between. Give our nation a compassionate heart, O Lord, for those who are starving and dying from the lack of basic sustenance. Please enable assistance for those in need, Lord. Let the hungry of the world be fed, the thirsty receive drink, the homeless find shelter, and the poor be uplifted. Let the evils of poverty be overcome, and help us to fight more intensely for special assistance for the needy. Amen.

For Those Needing Work

How discouraging it must be to want to work and earn a living but to be unable to find any work. Today, I pray for all those looking for a job, especially those who must have a job soon to keep them and their loved ones alive and well. All things are possible with you, O Lord. Lead people to jobs, Lord. Enable employers to provide jobs. Match up those looking for a job with those who are offering one, that our system of employment may support those in need. Some jobs seem to be just right, some are tedious, some are difficult, some are boring, and some are not very desirable. Yet all serve a purpose, and I pray that work will come to those who need it and that the work will provide income and resources. I am especially thinking of those I personally know who are looking for work. Lead them, help them, and grant them their desired jobs. Into your hands I commend those who want to work. Lord, please help them. Amen.

For Those in Our Military Services

In these times, many people and many spiritual groups are opposed to any kind of military actions. Many others, however, feel that military efforts are necessary to preserve and protect human rights. In the midst of controversy as to whether a war is justified or military action is necessary, citizens voluntarily give their time and energy and risk their lives to serve in our military forces. They prepare to follow the orders of our military leaders and, if necessary, to put themselves in harm's way for the cause. I pray for your protecting hand over these people, Lord. Keep them from suffering and from harm as they loyally serve for our benefit and for our national welfare. When harm is done to them, grant your healing presence and merciful support for their recovery. When conditions are terrible, grant them patience, bravery, and loyalty to sustain them. Grant wisdom and godly insight to our military leaders so that their decisions and actions will be just and will result in peacefulness. Amen.

For Faith for Another Person

The wonderful blessing of faith is so needed by this person to whom my heart goes out at this time. It is my sincere prayer that you, O Lord, will work faith in this person's heart. Faith is a divine gift—a miracle. It is impossible to receive faith without spiritual power, yet it is offered freely to all who will take it and believe by the empowering of the divine Spirit. It is not your will, Lord, that anyone should be without spiritual faith in your love, but unfortunately, a person can reject the invitation to faith and the holding on to faith. Break down all rejection and all evil force that would keep faith away from this person, O Lord. Exert your victory over sin and every evil that might stand in the way of faith in that person's heart. Begin your spiritual work—strengthen it, renew it, revitalize it, and do whatever is necessary, Lord, to bring spiritual faith to this person now. Help me to be an instrument for faith, if that is possible, Lord, so that my words and/or my actions may be used in your holy work. We all need faith in you to live and to die in peace and hope, so grant it now to this person's heart for whom I pray, according to your will. Amen.

For Someone's Success

None of us really deserves all of the good things we enjoy in this life, but it is your generous love and favor that enable us to be successful in our endeavors and gain our desires. I ask that you bless the ones for whom I am praying now, Lord. Bless them with good success to crown the efforts they have made, the work they have done, and the hopes they have expressed. Warm the hearts of those involved so that they will know that they are not the authors and finishers of their own accomplishments but that your will is in motion, and you are to be thanked for your love. Give those who are successful a celebration of joy in living, that a positive and responsible attitude may continue to encourage them and at the same time, keep them humble and thankful to you. So first, Lord, I pray for success . . . and then for a godly, right spirit within them. Amen.

Prayers of Thanksgiving

Thankful for Common Blessings

I am embarrassed, Lord, that I take so much for granted and often do not even recognize or remember how many good things I enjoy in this life. I often do not even think of the common things as blessings at the time, and I surely do not remember that they are products of your generous love. Lord, I am thankful for many little blessings—the kindness of a friend, the beauty of flowers, the smooth gelato flavors, the innocent words of a child, the sight of the full moon, the chirping of the crickets, the smell of a bakery, the taste of my favorite pie, someone's complimentary words, an automobile that gives me little trouble, convenience stores, a sale just when I need it, listening to the rain. And there are the ordinary things that give me joy because I can still do them—baking, shopping, reading, watching television shows, going to a movie, hearing a concert, taking a shower, going out to dinner, hugging a friend, visiting an old acquaintance, traveling, buying something new. I am so sorry that often I am unmindful of how many good things I enjoy. Right now my heart is overflowing with thanksgiving for the abundance of daily blessings—common, ordinary things. I am truly rich and blessed, and I love the good things of this life. Give me a thankful heart, O Lord. Amen.

Roy K. Bohrer

Rejoicing for Happiness

There's a *Peanuts* cartoon in which Lucy explains how we often feel "torn up," because the human heart has the forces of both good and evil in it, and they fight with each other. I am so thankful that for now, the good side is winning in me, and happiness is way up on top. This joy that has come to me is a wonderful blessing from your hand, O Lord, and I rejoice in my happiness because of it. All too often, it seems that evil is winning because it is so strong or because I let it take over, and unhappiness overtakes me. But happiness that comes with good news, good actions, good people, and good results is so much more to be desired, and it makes life so much more pleasant. I am blessed with happiness now, and I pray that I may hold on to these feelings of happiness as much as possible. It is what you want for your people and your world. Amen.

Thanks for Love

Spiritual leaders have always stressed love as the greatest good and the greatest blessing. I am so thankful that I have experienced love in my life. I have not always recognized it or known it was there, and I have not always accepted it. I am mindful and thankful that much love has come to me. First, there was God's love; it made me who I am and gave me life itself. My first human love probably came from family members, parents, grandparents, siblings, and various other relatives. Thank you, Lord, for family love in all of its forms and with all of its weaknesses. Through the years I have been blessed with the love of friends, and also with the blessing of a spouse or mate—a life partner—with whom the love is of the highest human commitment. There have been others who were close to me and really loved me—teachers, spiritual leaders, coworkers, caretakers. Thank you, Lord, for the love that came to me and that still does come from assorted people in my life. It is often unexpected, often unannounced, often unreturned, and too often unappreciated. I am also thankful that I have been able to give love, for it is more blessed to give love than to receive it. Thank you; I am truly blessed in love. Amen.

Thanks for Your Mercy

Your mercy, Lord, is the source of your forgiveness, and your forgiveness is what makes my life worthwhile. Thank you, Lord, for your mercy, for without it all my continuing failures of thought, word, and deed would make me a totally useless, unworthy person. It is a great mystery how, in mercy, you can offer us forgiveness for evil and accept us as good; how you do not turn your back on us because your desire is for our cleansing, healing, and redemption. It is a great mystery how you freely offer us the second chance, the third chance, and on and on in never-ending mercy; how you provide the sacrifice, the redemption, and the way of salvation for those who can never save themselves. Continue to give me faith in your mercy, Lord, and make me thankful for your daily eternal acceptance. Amen.

Thanks for All Things Beautiful

Whether I've thought about it or not, my world has been filled with beautiful things throughout the years. "Beauty is in the eye of the beholder," of course, so not all things are equally beautiful to all people—but that is good. As I give thanks for beauty in my world, I think of beautiful people, beautiful flowers, beautiful scenery, beautiful sounds that talented humans produce, beautiful animals, beautiful buildings, beautiful handicrafts and artworks, beautiful words from creative minds, beautiful homes and gardens, and beautiful foods and meals. There can be beautiful nights, beautiful lights, beautiful weather, beautiful performances, beautiful waters, and beautiful suns. I am so thankful that I have enjoyed beauty and still enjoy it. Do not let me forget. Thank you, Lord, for this wonderful joy. Amen.

Roy K. Bohrer

Thankfulness for My Parents

As we grew up and became adults, most of us saw the reality of our parents in their strengths and weaknesses and their failures and successes. For some reason in these later years of my life, I think of my parents more often than I did in earlier years, and I am thankful for them and everything they did for me. I am thankful for what they were, though imperfect, because I know they did the best that they could. They did as they thought was right and necessary, and your mercy, Lord, covers all of their flaws. I learned lessons from my parents—they taught some of them intentionally; others I just picked up along the way. I now have a forgiving spirit toward them. I can rest peacefully about the ups and downs of our relationship. I ask forgiveness for the ways in which I was not a good and helpful child and the ways in which I hurt or disappointed my parents. I am thankful for their sacrifices, their hard work, their determination, their faithfulness, and their good examples. Thank you, Lord, for my parents. Let their lives be a good memory for me. Amen.

Thanks for Friends

The help and support of friends along my way has been a blessing too great to measure. Some friends have been with me for nearly all of my life and others for short times, but I am thankful, Lord, for all whom I have called my friends. My friends have been through a lot with me. They have stuck by me, supported me, comforted me, rescued me, encouraged me, and lifted me up—sometimes literally. Friends have laughed with me, cried with me, played with me, worked with me, eaten with me, drunk with me, traveled with me, rested with me, scolded me, and complimented me. Thank you, Lord, for friends, because I can see that your action and presence has come to me through them. My friends have been God's instruments in my life. Whatever good my friends have done for me has been godly, because Lord, you have done it through them. It gives me pride and joy to remember my friends—the touches of God in my life. Amen.

Thanks for Family Members

They say you can choose your friends but not your family. That is true, but I have some family members who I would surely have chosen for myself, because they have been blessings for which I am very thankful. I am certainly not close to all of my relatives; I do not even know some of them. I am truly sorry for any of my failings regarding family bonds, my lack of attention or response, or my negligence or rejection. My human frailties and sins could surely have been barriers or the cause of weak connections or breakdowns in my family relationships, and I must ask for forgiveness for those. But I am praying in thankfulness now for those members of my family to whom I am connected with the bonds of love and support. Some of them are closer to me than anyone else. We have shared together. We have been together in many circumstances. We know and accept each other, and we celebrate our common family heritage as relatives. We can see ourselves in each other, and that is good, because it is evidence of our family tie. I seem to think more about family members in these older years—those who have passed away as well as those who are still here with me—and when I do, I am thankful that I have a family. Thank you, Lord, that there are other people who know me and care about me, because we have been connected by the ties of family. Amen.

Thanks for Answers and Completions

Not a day goes by without a difficulty to be fixed, a decision to be made, an effort to be started, or a question to be answered. I want to do the right things and make the right decisions, but I do not always want to rely on myself for these answers. Help me, Lord, with the decisions and answers that I need. Thank you for showing me the way and for leading me to do what I am supposed to do. Some of these things are small matters, and some are major issues, but they all tend to weigh me down and disturb my peacefulness in an unhealthy way. Strengthen my faith, Lord, and forgive my weakness of faith. Do not let me become burdened by the cares of the days or the questions of life. Give me the assurance that things will work out for good and will be completed in the right time. Remind me that evil cannot win the day, although it can cause grief, heartache, trouble, and confusion. Let me rest securely in these days, even though problems will hang on and questions will be unanswered for a time. At the right time, which is unknown to me, let the decisions be made. In my frail humanity, I cannot see and I cannot know. All of the best answers and completions lie in your divine wisdom. Let me not feel forsaken because, thankfully, I do not decide alone. Amen.

Thanks for Safety

I have been kept safe. I have made it safely, Lord, thanks be to you. Maybe my fears and my worries were a sign of weakness and were unfounded. Maybe there was not any danger or question, but it seems there is always a possibility of harm or error or trouble because there is so much evil in the world. I believe that you go with us, Lord, because we are yours. I believe that you help us through, whatever the degree of danger, because we put ourselves in your hands. I believe that as we invite you, we have your divine will and power present with us. I have been kept safe again, Lord. I can rejoice and be assured in my security with you. Amen.

Thanks for This Day

This is another day that you have made, Lord. I can rejoice and be glad in it. From the rising of the sun in the morning to its setting in the evening, this is another day of my life for which I thank you. This day has its promises, its possibilities, its opportunities, its expected blessings, and its unexpected joys. This day also has its warnings, its temptations, its pains, its losses, and its disappointments. We have such a good God to bless us abundantly, and we have such a strong force of evil that works against all good things. Help me again this day to see myself on the side of good, to fight against the forces of evil. Remind me again this day that the ultimate power and victory are with you, Lord. I will bless you and bless this day. I walk with you in thankfulness. Amen.

Thanks for Food and Drink

For many years I have had food to eat and enough to drink. I have just taken it for granted through the years, often without recognizing my food and drink as a blessing, a pleasure. Thank you, Lord, for providing me with my daily necessities of food and drink. In fact, I have often had more than enough—way more than enough. Forgive me the wasting of food and drink that I have sometimes done, especially when I think that many people have not had enough. I am blessed to have had many different foods and drinks throughout the years, in many different places and on many different occasions, prepared by many different cooks and shared with many different people. Although my aging body does not accept or adapt to different foods and drink as well as when I was younger, thanks be to you, O Lord, for food and drink throughout all these years and right up to today. Amen.

Thanks for Bringing Me Home

I have always liked returning home after being away, but now, in these senior years, I am happier than ever to be able to come back to my own place. Whether I am away just for a day or for a long trip, there is something comfortable and good about coming home to the place you have provided for me, Lord. Thank you, Lord, that I even have a place to stay, a place that is my home. It may be small; it may not be very fancy or well-supplied; it may not be the best place I have ever had; and it may not be what anyone else wants. But right now, this is my place. Thank you for bringing me safely home once again. Perhaps this coming-home feeling is a little prediction of the comfort and joy that there will be someday when you bring me to my eternal home with you. Let me never forget your presence with me here or your promise that I will be with you at home forever. Amen.

Prayers for Special Occasions

On the Death of a Friend or Loved One

Lord, help me to hold on to your promise that our times are in your hands. I feel so sad and confused about the passing of my friend/ loved one. Even though I know we all must depart, and sometimes it is a blessed relief from the troubles of this world, I have feelings of loneliness and sorrow and anger. Why did this person have to go? Why now? Can leaving this life of so many joys really be a blessing? Is there a plan? Forgive me, Lord, for my doubts and disbeliefs. Please comfort me and all who are grieved with your loving assurances and the gift of strong faith. Help us to keep good memories and rejoice in your forgiveness. Let us be thankful for the life that we shared with this friend/loved one and the times we had together. Keep me strong and keep me steady, Lord. I am thankful for your love and mercy. Amen.

On the Day of a Friend's or Loved One's Funeral

This is not a day to which I looked forward, Lord, and certainly I would not have planned to have this funeral today. I find it hard to let go of loved ones and to have to say a permanent earthly good-bye to those who meant so much to me. Pope John XXIII once said that any day is a good day to be born, and any day is a good day to die. In your mercy, that is surely true, and in light of your divine will, I know it. Lift me up today with the strength of your Spirit and the comfort of your love. Let me go through what I must. Let me be brave and face reality. Let me not sorrow, as those who have no hope, and help me to give a good witness of comfort for others. Especially at this time, give me the peace that passes all human understanding, because I am nothing unless I rest in your peace. Remind me that whether I live or die, I am the Lord's. I am yours. Amen.

On a Day of National Pride

"God bless our native land! Firm may she ever stand . . ." I am proud to be a citizen of this country and to live with the blessings we enjoy. If people from past centuries were alive today, they could not believe how much we enjoy in this life or how much "daily bread" we have. Thanks be to you, O Lord, for these undeserved blessings of our land. We do not need as much as we have. Help us, as a nation, to share and to give to the world, especially to those in need. Keep our nation secure and peaceful, with freedom for our religious practices, our daily activities, and our decisions. Give us good and wise leaders who will govern our nation to keep it healthy and strong. Help us to welcome others to become citizens of our country in an orderly and right way, so that they may also be blessed. Give us pride in our land, not in an ungodly or selfish way but in a loyal and thankful way, that we may always stand up for our nation and call upon you to bless it and keep it. Amen.

Roy K. Bohrer

In a Time for Spiritual Renewal

In our communities of faith, to assist us in our spiritual lives, we have designated special days and seasons as times for more intense spiritual application and spiritual renewal. Help me to focus on your love and my relationship as your child every day, Lord, but at this special time of spiritual emphasis, warm my heart even more with the knowledge of your presence and the peace of your mercy. Never let me forget how blessed I am to know you by faith and to enjoy walking and talking with you throughout my days. For so many years I have been blessed, O Lord, often without even thinking about it or acknowledging it. Forgive my times of being spiritually lukewarm and forgetful. When I am weak, support me. Where I am weak, show me a way for strengthening. It is not new faith that I need, Lord, but reminders, renewal, and rejuvenation in order to make me a better and more faithful person, one who will lead to more rejoicing in your love and salvation. Amen.

On a Day of New Beginnings

As with most older persons, Lord, I do not like changes. I am comfortable with things as they are, even if they aren't so good. But this is a day of newness for me—a new beginning, a new something. Thank you, Lord, that the future is in your hands. Help me to try to do my part—to be positive, to feel new, to do new things—but give me the faith to remember that I am not all-powerful. Do not let me reject change just because it is different. A new time, a new year, a new relationship, a new place, a new opportunity, a new responsibility, a new decision—whatever this is, Lord, go with me. Do not leave me or forsake me because, as a famous theologian once said, surely if I am left to myself, I will make a mess of it. Give me the assistance that I will need, O Lord. Throughout my years, I have faced something new many times, so this is not unusual. Help me to remember and call upon my past to encourage and assist me. Let me be at peace and rest securely. Amen.

On My Birthday

No matter how many years have passed, a birthday is still a special day to remember and maybe even celebrate. Thank you, Lord, for all of my years. Thank you for all the people who came into my life and were meaningful to me. Thank you for all the opportunities I have enjoyed, all the things I have done, and all the blessings you have showered upon me in abundance. For me, the years have gone by so quickly. How insignificant I am, and how very small is my little life in eternal terms! Nevertheless, you have assured your people that everyone is important to you, and every life is one that you have made and blessed for your purposes. O Lord, I hope I have fulfilled at least some of your purposes for me. Forgive me for what I have not done and for what I have done wrong. Now I begin another year of life. Who knows how many years I will have? In these days, many people seem to be living longer and staying healthier. Grant that to me, Lord, if that could be my blessing. In this coming year, give me the joy of living in your name. Keep me always close to you so that I may call upon you in faith, as a child relies upon a loving parent. In the palm of your hand is where I want to be—safe, secure, and content. Happy birthday to me! Amen.

On Someone Else's Birthday

God bless the person whose birthday I observe today, with the joy of celebration and a hopeful look toward the future. Help this person to use this birth-date anniversary as a time to reflect upon your goodness and love, with thankfulness for all that the years have brought. I thank you, Lord, for this life that you have given, which has been meaningful to many, including me. Give a freshness of faith and a sincerity of life on this birthday so that it may be a meaningful day of celebration and reflection. Do not let this person take for granted the time that is given or the opportunities encountered. Please give this dear person a wonderful and meaningful birthday commemoration, with joyful hope for the future of many years, in your name. Amen.

On a Retirement

Retiring from a job or profession is very important time for anyone, whether it has been many years in one position or there have been different positions and endeavors through the years. Retirement means a change—adjustments in time, finances, activities, maybe friendships, and maybe places. Lord, we need your guiding light and loving care in these changes and adjustments. Some things are within our control, and some things are a total mystery and out of our hands. Give us wisdom and insight to make the right decisions. Give us patience and understanding in making adjustments. Do not let us go astray down selfish pathways. Keep us from a feeling of uselessness, Lord, because as long as we have days to live, we have days to be useful and important in many ways, for others and for ourselves. Lord, keep us from becoming antisocial, disinterested, depressed, or isolated. As in all other times and with all other milestones, Lord, continue to uplift us with your love, strengthen us with your mercy, and sustain us with your presence. We walk on but never alone. Thank you, Lord. Amen.

On an Anniversary

Thank you, Lord, for the significance of this important anniversary date, this marker to remember an important past event. Thank you, Lord, for all of the time that this anniversary represents and all of the blessings that have come to us. Some days were not so good or peaceful, and some times were not so successful. Forgive us, Lord, for the evils that overtook us, the mistakes we made, and the ungodliness in us that reared its ugly head. Let us bask in the knowledge of your unending mercy and forgiveness that blankets our lives by faith. Let us be quick to know and use forgiveness among us. As we go forward from this milestone, continue to warm our hearts with your mercy and love so that we may cherish the time you give to us and make the best use of it. Sustain us with divine strength and power to meet whatever comes along so that the victories will be won and successes will be celebrated, and we can enjoy more happy anniversaries. This is the day that the Lord has made. Let us rejoice and be glad in it. From the rising of the sun to its setting, let the name of the Lord be praised. Amen.

Roy K. Bohrer

On New Year's Day

Happy New Year to me, Lord, and to all those I love and to all people everywhere! Happy New Year comes from your love and blessing, Lord, or it will not be happy at all. Thank you for giving us a new year, a turn of our earthly calendars to another year of life here. This is a time for review of the past year—for asking forgiveness for all that was wrong, all that went astray, all that was unloving, and all the times we indulged in evil. It is a time for new resolutions. Help us to be more loving, more vigilant for good, more just in our thinking and decisions, godlier in all ways, and stronger to fight temptations. I have particular problems and concerns, Lord, for which you know I need an extra measure of help. The years keep ticking away, as does my life. Who knows for how long? It is not for us to know the time or the season appointed by your almighty will. There is a time for everything under the sun. Lord, you have been our dwelling place for years and generations, and your promise to keep us forever is sure and certain. In faith, Lord, I face this new year, grateful to be alive for as long as you give me life in this wonderful world you have made. Amen.

On the Birth of a Child

There is nothing in this world as godly as creating life, because life was created first by you, Lord. There is no human power or joy that compares with the creation of a new life, the birth of a child. Thank you for the creative privilege you have shared with these parents as they have brought forth their new baby. Thank you for the successful delivery of this child into the world. May this child develop and grow in a healthy and strong way, physically, mentally, emotionally, and spiritually. Bring this child close to you and your love for all of his or her life, that this child may know the gift of salvation and the joy of service in your faith. Be with the parents as they strive to do what is good and right for their child, guiding them in their parental words and actions. Help them to realize the importance of their role and the significance of their influence for their child. Give to all of them the comfortable feeling of family for all of their days and the assurance of their spiritual family forever. Amen.

Remembering a Departed Loved One's Birthday

Thank you, Lord, that the memories of those we loved stay with us to comfort and uplift us for a long time after they are gone, maybe for the rest of our lives. As I remember the birthday of this dear loved one, I think about that life that was so important to me. The life of that person was a gift to me, Lord, one of your blessings that I still cherish and am thankful for to this very day. It is a great gift that I can remember the influence this person had on me and the many good things we shared. I enjoy the gift of remembering the days we spent together, as well as the sorrowful times when we supported each other. Help me to remember good times and good things to encourage me. Today, deliver me from sad grieving and unnecessary remorse, and give me peacefulness in the memories that I have. A birthday is a time to celebrate, as this loved one and I did when we were together. On this day, let me celebrate our life together, our loving relationship, and the joys we shared. My heart feels happy birthday. Amen.

At the Time of a Family Reunion or Gathering

Sometimes I feel that a family gathering is meaningful and fun, and sometimes I feel it is painful and unreal. This does not mean, though, that it is not an occasion for blessings. Lord, do not let my negative feelings get in the way of some important sharing and joy in our family get-together. Do not let my attitude keep me from going to the gathering and participating. I am not sure why getting together with some of my family is unpleasant or embarrassing or annoying. I don't know if it is my problem or theirs. For better or for worse, everyone there is a family member, whether someone is similar to or different from me, successful or unsuccessful, or have bad habits or good personalities. Keep me from feelings of superiority or inferiority or exclusiveness. Let me see all of my family members as people who are in need of love and acceptance. Help me to go to the gathering with a positive attitude of sharing and learning. Let me be seen as someone who is a blessing to others in whatever I say and do and in my acceptance of all. Help me to mirror your love for all of creation and for all people. Use me as an instrument for good. Bless this gathering with positive and joyful feelings and important family sharing. Amen.

Prayers for Times and Days

On a Sunday

Although it is actually the first day of the week, Sunday generally feels as if it's the end of the week—a special day to celebrate and rejoice in the Lord's goodness. These days, Lord, I often do not have the privilege and joy of community worship, and I cannot enjoy Sunday as a family-gathering day, as was often true in the past. Forgive me, Lord, that now Sunday is often a day of depression and sadness for me. When I am able to attend, or gather, or join in fellowship, let me be thankful for blessings. Help me to enjoy Sunday as a special day whenever I can. When I am not with anyone else on a Sunday, still let me be thankful for the blessings of my life. Changes have come for me, for my family, and for my friends, but do not let these changes weigh me down. Be with those who still gather this day—communities of faith, families, friends—and bless them with happiness. I keep the faith, Lord; help me to apply it. Amen.

On a Monday

For so many of my years, this was the first day of the school week or the first day of the working week—a day of beginnings. Sometimes it was exciting, and sometimes it was dreaded. Now I know, Lord, that I should have rejoiced in the new beginnings of every week, because now I could use some new-beginnings excitement. Help me to keep my mind and body alive to some newness, especially on a Monday. Thank you for all the years in which I was busy and active, and keep me alert to the blessings of opportunities that come to me. Let me see in this week the chance to do something new or to learn something new, and give me the willpower to do it. Amen.

On a Tuesday

As it's still early in the week, on Tuesday I can make plans for this week—to accomplish something, to fulfill some goal. Do not let me fall into the slump of nameless days or useless weeks, but push me, Lord, to continue a schedule, to make plans, and to set my mind to activities. I am thankful for the abilities, opportunities, and resources that I still have to apply to these days, and I need your help, Lord, to sort out what I should do. Keep me in tune with your will and the ways of the world so that I am not a stranger to those around me or to your presence. Amen.

On a Wednesday

Keep me going, Lord, on this day that is midway in the week. Help me to remember enough of the past that it is useful to my good nature, and keep me looking forward enough to be alert to my needs and opportunities. Help me to sort out the good from the bad, the right from the wrong, the helpful from the destructive in this confusing world. Give me the faith that this world is still not such a bad place to be and that as long as I am here, there are blessings for me to enjoy and tasks for me to do, wherever I am. My times are in your hands, O Lord, and that is a good thing, because often I do not know what to expect or do. Help me to walk by faith. Amen.

On a Thursday

Time still keeps marching on; often, it seems to go quite fast. This week's days are going by, and I am getting through them. Even though people think I have all the time in the world to do anything, often I am not able to do everything I wish. Thank you, Lord, for your continuous mercy in keeping me going, your grace in lifting me up, and your love in supporting me. When I was younger, I did not think much about your daily help and presence, but now I can see that you walk with me all the way. How wonderful is your forgiveness to cover my flaws, my sins, and my weaknesses! You have given me this day—and every day—my daily bread! How small I am, and how great you are! Amen.

Roy K. Bohrer

On a Friday

The end of the week is upon us, Lord, and I thank you for whatever good has been in this week, whatever good has come to me, and whatever good I have been able to do. Never let me lose my awareness of blessings or my thankful heart. I rejoice with those who have had a productive and successful week at their work, and pray they will have an enjoyable weekend. Fridays were always a day of special joy—the completion of another week—and I am thankful, Lord, that I have seen another week in this world. Forgive my complaining, my lack of trust, my mistakes, my misjudgments, and my faithlessness. Some things never change, and there will never be a time when I do not need a big helping of forgiveness, in your mercy. Keep before me the vision of my worthiness because of your love and my importance as your child, so that I can continue to go forward in confidence. Amen.

On a Saturday

The last day of the week, the day on which you rested from the creation of all things and gave us all time to take a break and rejoice in the world and everything in it. For many, this day is a day of rest, a day of worship. This day is a reminder that an ending time is a great time to reevaluate, to renew, to repair, to refresh, to rethink, and to revitalize. Saturday happens every week for this reason, but we are reminded that the end of all weeks is coming some time—maybe soon—so we are to use the ending time for our renewal and for the preparation of what is to come. What has the past week meant, and what will the coming week mean? Saturday, the day of refreshment and rededication to the rest of the days, points us to the time of rededication for the end of all time. Even so, come, Lord! Amen.

In Spring

Thank you, Lord, for the freshness of new life in the springtime. Springtime has forever been a sign of your creating love and power. Mankind has researched and answered many mysterious questions, but how could any human have figured out how to make a baby bird or a new oak tree and put them in the right places? How marvelous are your works in all creation, O Lord. And then there is new spiritual life. Desperation can turn into dedication. Sin can be forgiven. A human spirit can find the Spirit of God and live forever. Thank you for springtime and for all new life. Thank you for my new life in you, Lord. I rejoice in another springtime, a sign of newness and life and love. Amen.

In Summer

The new life begun in spring grows up to the warmth of the sun and the washing of rain. Where there are those who need warmth to grow, grant it to them, O Lord. Where there are those who need important rain, grant it to them, O Lord. It has been many years since I first became a grown-up, Lord, but I remember the importance of good nurturing and loving care. Not only for the world of nature during this summer but also for people, Lord, I pray that there will be plenty of nurturing, love, and growth. In this summertime, warm my heart, Lord, so that I may be alert to the needs of other people, quick to forgive, and eager to share, and that I may be full of love. It is not too late for me to grow, so lead me to new possibilities or better ways or richer times, that there may be a fine harvest. Amen.

In Autumn

How I love the smell of autumn air, the gentleness of autumn sunshine, the cooler evenings, and the colors. Thank you, Lord, for bringing the autumn harvest time—the culmination of spring life and summer growth. Autumn is full of celebrations and harvest festivals that attest to the abundance of your love, Lord. Make us thankful people who notice and appreciate the abundance of our blessings. Of course, autumn reminds us of the slowing down of life, as plants begin to wilt, dry up, and die away. I see in autumn what happens to people—wilting, weakening, and finally death. I don't know if I am still in the harvest time, when I can enjoy the produce of the life for which I have prepared. Or am I closer to that time of wilting and death? It is not for us to know the time that you have appointed, Lord, and I am ready for whatever the time will bring. Whether I live or die, I am with you, Lord. Amen.

In Winter

Cold wind, low temperatures, shorter days, and more darkness mark winter; there is no more growth, and life comes to a standstill. There is a time for everything, and this is the time for death. Let me learn the lesson of winter, Lord—that life will not continue here on this earth forever. In a way, all of my life has been a preparation for the end, because time marches on through its periods of newness and growth and harvest and death. I know that the human body starts dying from the time it is born. Lord, let me not be surprised or despondent at the deterioration of old age or the impending signs of death. I can face the end with the assurance of peace and hope—to sleep with my forebears and inherit the promises of eternity. Winter is not a dreadful time, because during winter we can enjoy the fruits of harvest and the good things that came from the previous seasons. I look forward to the winter of eternal life, out of this world, when I will inherit a time of great joy that my ears and eyes cannot imagine. Continue to uphold me with the joy of my salvation. Amen.

Roy K. Bohrer

At Close of Day

It has been said that every night's sleep is a "little death," as our bodies shut down. I am ready to rest from this day, Lord, as I thank you for all of the good that has happened and has come to me today. I also ask forgiveness for all of the bad that I have done this day. No matter how hard I try, no day is perfect. Now, I rest in your grace and mercy. Help me to have a good and peaceful sleep this night, O Lord, that I may wake up refreshed. Give respite to my aging muscles and nerves and organs and bones; give freedom from pain and strength for the next day. Clear my mind of all worries, guilt, and concerns, and help me to relax. Let me feel your hand of blessing upon my head and my whole body. If anyone is concerned about me tonight, give peacefulness and love to calm that person. Make me ready for whatever tomorrow will bring. If tomorrow, for me, is not in this world, Lord, I am ready to go into your eternal love and blessing; just take me. I rest in peace tonight. Amen.

At Night

Now I lay me down to sleep,
I pray the Lord my soul to keep.
If I should die before I wake,
I pray the Lord my soul to take.
If I should live for many days,
I pray the Lord to guide my ways.
Amen.

At Beginning of Day

Blessed are you, O Lord, that I am given another day to live on this earth. This is a day that the Lord has made. I will rejoice and be glad in it. From the rising of the sun to its setting, let the name of the Lord be praised. Today brings me time and opportunity to do things, to say things, to influence people, and to do some good, so help me, Lord. Help me to fight against whatever evils may attack me this day and to bear whatever pains I may have. Let me be a witness to your love and your mercy whenever I can, that I may be an instrument of bringing your kingdom to the hearts and lives of people. Lord, let me be an instrument of peace to others. May I be a blessing to those I meet today. I commit this day into your care and mercy. Amen.

In the Morning

This new day I awake from sleep,
I pray the Lord my soul to keep.
If today I am called to die,
I pray the Lord take me home on high.
If I should live for many days,
I pray the Lord to guide my ways.
Amen.

Praying with Others,
Prayer Aids

A Five-Point Form of Prayer to Memorize as a Help When Asked to Say a Short Prayer Aloud

1. *Address*: O Lord / Dear God / Heavenly Father

2. *Descriptive Phrase That Fits the Topic of This Prayer*: Who knows all things / You never leave us / You have all power

3. *Thanksgivings*: Offer thanks for blessings in the past / thanks for friends and family / thanks for faith / thanks for the peace of forgiveness

4. *Petitions*: Whatever you want to ask for in this prayer

5. *Closing*: In the name of the Lord, amen. / With confidence, amen. ("Amen" means "yes, surely it will be.")

Sample prayer: (1) O Lord God, (2) you are the only one with all power and all knowledge. (3) We thank you for the good health that this dear lady has enjoyed, that you have kept her and all of us in your love and that you have given us faith, especially for our hard times. (4) Now we ask that you will bring healing power to this dear lady. Bless the work and the decisions of the doctors. Give her a strong faith and a peaceful outlook, and keep us all strong in love and faith. (5) Confident in your mercy and love, we can be assured of your help. Amen.

A Simple Method to Help Remember for Whom to Pray: Praying the Fingers of Your Hand

1. Thumb (closest to your heart)—pray for those who are closest to you.

2. Index finger (pointer)—pray for those who point the way: teachers, pastors, counselors, doctors.

3. Middle finger (tallest)—pray for all leaders: government leaders on every level, church leaders, social leaders, those to whom you "look up."

4. Fourth finger (weakest)—pray for all who are weak in any way: those who are suffering, ill, troubled, or dying.

5. Little finger (smallest, least significant)—pray for yourself.

Turn the Spoken Prayer of One Person into a Group Prayer

The person speaking the prayer pauses after each of the sentences. or petitions, and the entire group then says a phrase together, such as "Lord, hear us," "This is our prayer," or "Hear our prayer." In this way, the entire group is involved, and the prayer becomes the prayer of the whole group.

Finis

O Lord, support us all the day long of this troublous life, until the shadows lengthen and the evening comes, and the fever of life is over, and our work is done.
Then in thy great mercy, grant us a safe lodging, a holy rest, and peace at the last. Amen.

(attributed to John Henry Cardinal Newman)

About the Author

Roy Kenneth Bohrer was born in 1938 and raised in the south suburbs of the Twin Cities in Minnesota. He received his bachelor of arts degree from the University of Minnesota, Minneapolis, and his master of divinity degree from Concordia Theological Seminary, Springfield, Illinois. While serving as pastor of Christ Lutheran Church in Austin, Texas, his interest in seniors and his understanding of their needs led to the beginning of a senior program and a specialized senior ministry. He was a popular instructor at senior centers and a spokesman and representative for citywide senior activities. Serving as the chairman and a member of the board of directors for several senior programs in the city of Austin, Roy received much recognition for his work with senior citizens, including the State of Texas Volunteer Commendation.

With his caring concern for seniors and his experience with senior interests, Roy also became a leader of retirement preparation seminars, assisting people in the honest expression of their needs and desires and their realistic planning for the senior years. Following his church ministry, for a number of years he was the executive director of several state and national professional nonprofit associations.

In preaching, teaching, addressing assemblies, and interpersonal relationships during his professional life, as well as in individual visitation and consultation, Roy was respected and appreciated for his right-on expressions, personable manner, and direct, easy-to-understand wording. He continues that manner of communication in these prayers. In addition to his now being a senior himself, his many years of ministry and volunteer service with seniors well qualify him for choosing the right topics and the appropriate wording for the variety of prayers in this book. Those who read advance copies have noted: "He knows what he is talking about," and "These prayers really fit my life."

Now retired, Roy lives in Austin, Texas. He travels frequently, visits with seniors on a personal basis, and volunteers with Mended Hearts (a national nonprofit organization that offers encouragement to heart disease patients and their families). He is enjoying his senior years by keeping active with various endeavors, including writing. His three children and two grandchildren all live close enough for frequent visits and intergenerational reality checks.

LEN ROY LORRAINE